TOMB RAIDERS

Discovering Tutankhamun

Simon Cheshire

Illustrated by Jim Eldridge

OXFORD
UNIVERSITY PRESS

Great Clarendon Street, Oxford OX2 6DP

Oxford University Press is a department of the University of Oxford.
It furthers the University's objective of excellence in research, scholarship,
and education by publishing worldwide in

Oxford New York

Auckland Cape Town Dar es Salaam Hong Kong Karachi
Kuala Lumpur Madrid Melbourne Mexico City Nairobi
New Delhi Shanghai Taipei Toronto

With offices in

Argentina Austria Brazil Chile Czech Republic France Greece
Guatemala Hungary Italy Japan Poland Portugal Singapore
South Korea Switzerland Thailand Turkey Ukraine Vietnam

Oxford is a registered trade mark of Oxford University Press
in the UK and in certain other countries

British Library Cataloguing in Publication Data

Data available

ISBN-10: 0 19 919 641 9
ISBN-13: 978 0 19 919641 8

5 7 9 10 8 6 4

Mixed Pack (1 of 6 different titles): ISBN 0 19 919647 8
Class Pack (6 copies of 6 titles): ISBN 0 19 919646 X

Illustrated by Jim Eldridge c/o Linda Rogers Associates
Cover photo by Amos Nachoum/Corbis Uk Ltd.

Acknowledgements
p4 Robert Holmes/Corbis UK Ltd.; pp4/5 Corel; p5 Dean
Conger/Corbis UK Ltd.; p9 Bettmann/Corbis UK Ltd.; p20
Bettmann/Corbis UK Ltd.; p23 Vanni Archive/Corbis UK Ltd.;
p24 Stapleton Collection/Corbis UK Ltd.; p25 Peter Clayton;
p11 Mary Evans Picture Library; p17 H Burton/Griffith Institute;
p19 Peter Clayton; p50 H Burton/Griffith Institute; p54 Fulvio
Roiter/Corbis UK Ltd.; p57 Gianni Dagli Orti/Corbis UK Ltd.;
p58 AKG – London; p60 Roger Wood/Corbis UK Ltd.; p62 Neil
Beer/Corbis UK Ltd.; pp62/63 Corel; p63 Griffith Institute.

Printed in China

Contents

Introduction

For many years, adventurers searched Egypt for ancient treasures. The pharaohs, who were the kings of ancient Egypt, had been buried with fabulous riches all around them. The ancient Egyptians believed that their pharaohs would need possessions in the **Afterlife**, so they were buried with all their favourite ornaments. The Egyptians also believed that a pharaoh would need his body in the Afterlife and so they **mummified** their dead rulers, and left food and drink with them.

Valley of the Kings, Egypt

They were then ready for their journey beyond death.

The precious things sealed up in the tombs attracted robbers. Many tombs were broken open and stripped clean just a few years after they were sealed. Others were plundered in more recent times. When archaeologists came to study ancient Egypt at the beginning of the 20th century, they found relatively little was left. No tomb had ever been found complete and undisturbed. That was, until November 1922...

A guide stands by an ancient **sarcophagus**

The Waterboy

The waterboy scurried across the rubble. He was only nine or ten years old, but he was the most important person on the whole site. No doubt about it. Without a waterboy like him, the workers could die of thirst. Oh yes, he was the main man around here, that was for sure.

"You! Waterboy! Here! Now!"

"Yessir!" cried the waterboy. He
scurried faster. The workers wanted a
drink. "Yessir, coming, yessir!"

The rubble beneath his thin sandals
was rocky and uneven. More than once
he nearly stumbled.

The entire valley was like that. Strewn

with rocky fragments that kicked up choking puffs of dust as you trudged across them. *The Valley of the Kings*, the Europeans called it. "The Valley of Heat and Flies more like," the waterboy thought. Although it was only a few kilometres from the banks of the Nile, the valley could have been a million years from anywhere. It was surrounded by high hills, and from the startlingly blue sky shone a merciless and unblinking sun.

The sun heated the rocks, and the rocks were dug away by the workers, local men hired by Mr Carter. All over the valley, the entrance to ancient tombs had been dug out, and now the waterboy was supposed to be helping to unearth another. Maybe. Or maybe not. They'd found nothing for months.

He looked over at Mr Carter, who was sitting on a rock, on his own. He liked

Howard Carter

Mr Carter. He treated his workers well, and he spoke the local language, unlike most of the archaeologists who came here searching. Carter was a tall man, dressed in a smart but dusty suit, with a hat firmly on his head to guard against the sun, and a thick black moustache drooping around his mouth. The waterboy couldn't help feeling that Mr Carter looked sad and nervous that day.

Howard Carter gave the waterboy a
brief smile and a nod, and the waterboy
wandered off to do some digging of his
own for a while. Carter was indeed
feeling depressed. For years, the experts
in London had been saying that the
Valley of the Kings was finished. No
more tombs to be discovered. No more
treasure to be found. No more to be
learnt.

But Carter was convinced that the
experts were wrong. He was determined

to sweep the valley from one end to the other. He was sure – absolutely sure – that the tomb of the boy pharaoh was here somewhere. The young king, who had died mysteriously all those thousands of years ago. Forget what the experts said. Carter had a nose for this kind of work and...

...Nothing had been found. Carter watched his men digging at the rocky soil. They didn't know what he knew. That this was his last chance. That if nothing was found soon, then digging would cease. The money and the patience of Carter's wealthy patron, Lord Carnarvon, were at an end. Carter had to make discoveries now, or he'd never get the chance to look again.

Sixteen Steps

The only sounds, echoing against the hills, came from the digging of the workmen. Chipping, shovelling, scraping, clearing.

As Carter watched and worried, the waterboy idly scratched at the soil. The rubble felt sharp and hot beneath his hands. His palms were thick with dust. He crouched, sweeping aside the dirt. More dirt beneath. And then more dirt. And then more. And then something hard.

Something flat.

The waterboy swept faster, ignoring the sharpness of the stones. It was something wide, and flat, and made of stone.

He looked up, shielding his eyes from the fierce glare of the sun. "Mr Carter!" he yelled. "Mr Carter!"

Carter jumped to his feet and hurried over. Voices started up all around. Workmen stopped digging and looked towards the waterboy, who was beckoning wildly for people to come over and look.

"Probably found a fragment of a pot," they mumbled to themselves.

The waterboy dug at the earth with his hands. He could feel his heart pounding. Only minutes before, he'd been feeling that the search was pointless, but now... anything could happen.

Howard Carter joined him. "Could be the top of a larger structure," said Carter, brushing sand aside frantically.

It was a step.

There was a flat surface, so smooth it must have been manmade. Along one edge, the stone turned downwards, into the ground.

Carter ordered the workmen to dig here. The waterboy stood back. Dozens of spades were aimed at the area in front of the step. Dazzling sunlight threw twisting shadows on the ground as they worked. However tired they were feeling, they dug as quickly as they could. This could be a find. This could mean bonus payments for all of them!

Soon a second step had been cleared.

It was definite. Steps leading underground.

Carter could hardly contain his excitement. "No, don't get your hopes up yet," he told himself. It might be nothing. It might be nothing of importance.

Or it might be the one tomb he'd

spent years looking for.

As fast as the heat of the day would allow, the workmen dug – as fast as buckets of earth could be moved away from the steadily growing hole in the ground.

One step after another. Down, and down. Until there were sixteen.

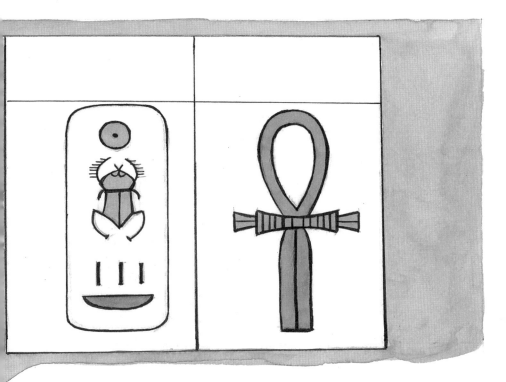

And below ground level, at the foot of the staircase, was a large plaster block, taller than a man. Across its rough surface were... markings...?

Carter took a closer look. They were the imprints of ancient Egyptian **hieroglyphics**. Great age, and the roughmaterial of the plaster, meant that they couldn't be read clearly.

But they were clearly there. This was an ancient hiding place of some sort, that much was certain.

The workmen and the waterboy stood in a jostling crowd at the top of the stone steps. They chattered together hurriedly, in hushed voices, about the possibilities of discovery and the merits of disturbing the resting places of the dead. The waterboy flicked his hair from his eyes with a grimy hand. Talk of disturbing the dead worried him, but

the workmen didn't seem concerned.
Their thoughts were on their bonuses.
This was going to be a good day for
them, too.

Carter took off his hat and fanned his
face for a moment or two. Flies buzzed
around his head and he swatted them
away.

Now was a time for clear, careful
thought. The proper thing to do would
be to summon Lord Carnarvon to the
site, and tell him of the find. Carter
dashed back up the steps.

The Boy King

Lord Carnarvon

Lord Carnarvon was an old man. His wealth normally gave him a comfortable life, but nothing could protect him from the scorching temperatures of the Egyptian desert.

"This had better be worth it, Carter, m'boy," he grumbled. "It's a long trek here from the hotel on the other side of the Nile." He turned and called to his travelling companion, his daughter Lady Evelyn Herbert, who was lagging a few metres behind. "Come along, girl! Chop chop!"

Lady Evelyn mumbled something that nobody else heard. She hitched up her calf-length skirts a little further and tottered awkwardly across the rubble of the valley.

"I hope we're going to be back for lunch, father," she called. "I simply

can't stay out in these conditions a moment more than necessary!"

Carter was hurrying over to the excavation. Carnarvon stopped for a moment, to order the waterboy to attend to the horses. The waterboy grumbled under his breath. He too wanted to see what had been found with everyone else, not look after the horses.

Carnarvon followed Carter down the staircase. Carter was already impatient to proceed. He beckoned to the old man hurriedly. Carnarvon made his way down the rock-strewn steps as fast as he could. As he arrived at the foot of the staircase, Carter was pointing out markings on the plaster wall.

"The design is certainly from the Eighteenth **Dynasty** of the pharaohs," said Carter. "You see the shape of the **cartouches**, the ovals which contain the hieroglyphs? At first, I thought that it could be the tomb of a noble. Or perhaps a store for the royal family. But then..."

"Then what?" said Carnarvon quietly, sitting on the steps and dabbing his brow with a handkerchief. He paused for a moment, suddenly realising what Carter meant. "So you've found a name?"

A cartouche from the tomb of Ramesses II

Lord Carnarvon, Lady Evelyn, and Howard Carter at the entrance to the tomb of Tutankhamun

Lady Evelyn appeared at the top of the steps. For the first time, she saw the wall-seal marked with ancient writing. As the strangeness of the place enveloped her, she almost forgot about the hot and tiring journey. Almost.

"Did we bring a hamper with us?" she called. "We're definitely not going to be back at the hotel in time for lunch, are we?"

Carter paid no attention to what she was saying. He looked at Carnarvon steadily.

"We have a name," he said. He dusted down the lower part of the plaster. "Look. The impressions are better preserved down here. See this one? Nine slaves, beneath the picture of a jackal. And here, three sets of symbols spelling out the name of the pharaoh."

Figure of a bird flanked by a cartouche spelling out Tutankhamun

Lord Carnarvon squatted down and peered at the hieroglyphs with screwed-up eyes. "Can't get close enough, m'boy. Not with m'back playing up. You'll have to translate for me."

Carter pointed to the three sets of symbols, one after the other. "Tut... Ankh... Amun..."

Carnarvon sat back on the steps. He put out a hand to steady himself. "Good Lord," he whispered. "The boy king! This is the tomb you've been searching for all these years. Tutankhamun."

Carter pointed to the top left corner of the plaster. "It's not all good news. Up there, can you see?"

There was a triangular section in the corner which looked different from the rest. Smoother, whiter.

"Grave robbers?" said Carnarvon.

Carter nodded. "In ancient times, I believe. If the tomb had been robbed more recently, we'd have already found evidence of it. There may be something left inside, though. The robbers wouldn't have bothered to re-seal a completely empty tomb."

"Then let's not delay," said Carnarvon. "Evelyn! Stop getting in the way up there, girl! Let the diggers through!"

The plaster seal was demolished. Beyond it was a square-shaped corridor, sloping downwards, packed to the roof with chippings of limestone. Carter

noticed with growing dismay that a
tunnel had obviously been made
through the chippings, in the top left
corner of the corridor. Someone had
been there before them.

He turned to his men. "Let's get it
clear!"

For hours they toiled. The sun slowly
moved across the sky. Long, jagged

shadows moved like broken fingers
through the valley, through the thick,
dust-filled air. The burnt orange glow of
late afternoon bathed the steps leading
to the tomb.

Up the steps came workers laden with
full buckets. Down the steps went
workers with empty buckets. A steady,
unending parade, up and down, down
and up.

As the sun began to sink behind the
hills, they found the second seal. Exactly
like the first, a thick plaster block across
the corridor.

Carter rushed to examine it. The corridor was long, and what daylight was left could barely reach this far underground.

He took out a short candle, struck a match, and ran the faint glow from the tiny flame across the surface of the plaster. Here were hieroglyphs again, the same as on the first seal, but far better preserved.

Carter's fingers delicately traced the outlines of the hieroglyphs. The light from the candle shuddered. He realised his hand was shaking.

Howard Carter and helpers opening the tomb of Tutankhamun

All across the plaster: Tut... Ankh... Amun... Tut... Ankh... Amun...

Tut... Ankh... Amun... And again, in the top left corner, signs that someone, long ago, had dug a hole and crawled through to the chamber beyond.

"What d'you think's behind this wall?" said Carnarvon. His voice echoed in the stone corridor. Lady Evelyn, inching cautiously along the corridor from the steps, shivered nervously despite the sticky heat.

Carter shrugged. "We can see that someone's been in here, so it's most probably an empty room. Of course, beyond that there may be rooms with a few items left behind. All in all, it's still an important archaeological find."

Carter took a trowel from one of the workmen and began to dig into the plaster. For minutes there was only the sound of metal scratching at the seal. Chunks of plaster dropped to the stone floor of the corridor in swirling gusts of dust. Carnarvon and Lady Evelyn stared nervously at Carter, Carnarvon holding out the candle so that Carter could see what he was doing. Nobody said a word. There were only the sounds of Carter hard at work, and an unbearable tension.

Lady Evelyn hardly dared to breathe. Partly, this was because of the thick, eye-stinging curtain of dust that hung in the air. Partly, it was fear of the unknown. Whether this tomb had been robbed or not, it was still a tomb. Slow, cold feelings of dread crept along her spine, just as they would have done if they had been digging up a grave back home in England.

"I'm through!" hissed Carter. His voice sounded loud and dense in the stuffy atmosphere of the corridor.

Wonderful Things

The candle flickered. Air from inside the tomb streamed out through the hole Carter had made, like a last gasp that had been held in tightly for

thousands of years. The explorers' lungs filled with the stinking, particle-filled air that had been entombed inside for so many centuries. They coughed hoarsely.

Carter held the candle to the hole, to test for poisonous gases. More than once in the past, archaeologists and adventurers had been overcome by the foulness of ancient tomb-air.

"I think it's safe," he whispered at last. "The chamber can't be filled with rocks, like this corridor was, or the air wouldn't have escaped like that."

"Look inside, m'boy," said Carnarvon. "Can you see if the room is very large?"

Carter moved up close to the hole he had made in the wall. Hot air was still flowing from inside. It brushed against his face. The hole was a ragged, black shape. And beyond it...?

Carter took the candle. Carefully, slowly, so as not to put out the flame, he pushed it through the hole. Grit and plaster fragments edged inside his sleeve as his arm slid forward.

View of the Antechamber with stacked up objects and broken items. Had someone been there before?

Moments later, he was holding the candle up inside the chamber, peering past his arm to see into the darkness.

At first, he could see nothing. The glow from the candle was faint and shifting. But as his eyes grew accustomed to the gloom, shapes began to emerge.

Shapes. Animals. Statues. Furniture.

And all reflecting the candlelight with the glowing shine of gold.

Everywhere.

"Carter!" called Carnarvon. "What can you see? What can you see?"

Carter could hardly speak. "Wonderful things," he whispered at last. "Wonderful things."

Night had fallen. The workmen at the surface were as amazed and delighted as Carter himself as news spread across the valley. But it had been a very long day. Little more could be accomplished until daybreak, and the excavation of a find as significant as this would take planning, and expertise, and equipment.

Everyone went home for the night. Carter, Carnarvon and Lady Evelyn returned to Carter's Arab-style house at the edge of the Valley of the Kings. He'd designed it himself, and called it Castle Carter.

Howard Carter's Arab-style house at Thebes

None of them anticipated getting any sleep. Then their nerves were stretched to breaking point, when they discovered a sluggish cobra in Carter's living room, a fresh meal forming a slowly digesting lump in its coiled body. It had eaten Carter's pet bird.

"Filthy beast," grumbled Carnarvon.

"It's just doing what it does to survive," mumbled Carter. "From the look of that snake, my poor bird was bitten about an hour ago."

"The moment when we broke into the tomb," said Lady Evelyn. "Father, I'm getting frightened. They say these ancient tombs are cursed."

"Steady on, girl," said Carnarvon, feeling rather unsteady.

"Superstitious nonsense," said Carter. "The local people don't believe in all that curse business. It's us Europeans who like to make up silly stories. We have to deal in facts. And the facts are that this could be the find of the century."

"I agree," said Carnarvon. "We have to handle the situation very carefully."

"Something like this can't be kept quiet," nodded Carter. "There's never been a find like it before. It could make headline news across the world. Before we know it, the valley will be swarming with people. We have to get the Egyptian authorities on our side and make sure things are done our way. So we must work out exactly what we've got down there. As soon as possible."

"I'll telegraph the museums in London and New York first thing tomorrow," said Carnarvon. "Get them to send out their top chaps."

Carter paused for a moment. "I was thinking... rather sooner than that. I was thinking we should take a closer look tonight."

"Tonight?" gasped Lady Evelyn. "On our own? In the dark? Down there? You must be mad!"

"We have **electric torches**," said Carter. "We have our knowledge of the ancient Egyptians to guide us. What we don't have is time."

5

A Pair of Eyes

In the dead of night, the valley was cold
and still. The heat of the day had
vanished completely, replaced by a dry
chill. Several miles away, the young
waterboy had been tucked up in his bed
for hours. He would have kicked himself
if he'd known what he was missing.

Down the stone steps of the tomb,
along the long, echoing corridor went
the three explorers. Each carried a
brightly shining flashlight which threw
a wide beam across the walls. The sound
of their footsteps seemed unbearably
loud.

Carter dug at the wall. Before long, he'd made a gap large enough for them all to crawl through.

The room was about eight metres wide, four metres deep. Its walls were plain stone. Their feet were the first to touch the chamber's floor in thousands of years. Yet there was an oil lamp in one corner, and the clear mark of a fingerprint in the paint on a statue. A

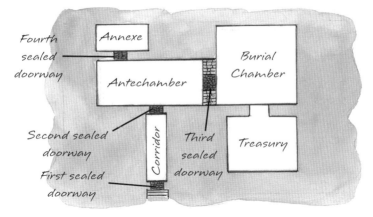

Plan of Tutankhamun's tomb

withered, dry-as-bone garland of flowers had been placed in front of the doorway they had just broken through. It was as if the tomb had been sealed only yesterday.

"I feel like we shouldn't be here," whispered Lady Evelyn.

They aimed their torches this way and that. There were three huge, gilt couches directly in front of them, surrounded by decorated boxes, carved figures, golden objects of every kind. The horns of a sacred ox sculpture shone out of the darkness.

To the left were the broken remains of chariots. Broken by the ancient tomb robbers. In the far corner of the room, beneath one of the couches, was a hole leading into a small **annexe** chamber. The annexe was a chaotic mess of smashed odds and ends.

"The robbers must have come in much as we did," said Carter, pointing his torch into the annexe. "Then they stole everything in this annexe and left, re-sealing the entrance. They must have intended to come back, but something stopped them. Perhaps they were killed for the treasures they'd already taken. Perhaps the location of this tomb was lost for some reason. Either way, it's to our great good fortune."

Suddenly Lady Evelyn gasped. She almost dropped her torch in fright.

To the right hand side of the main chamber was a third seal, blocking off another room. To either side of the seal were tall, black, wooden statues, dressed in gold, facing each other.

"Guardians," whispered Carter.

"Guarding what?" breathed Lady Evelyn.

Between the guardians was a richly

decorated **casket**. Carter and Carnarvon lifted it to one side and stood before the third seal.

In the sharp torchlight, their faces were a maze of light and dark. Their breathing echoed off the ceiling.

Carter began to dig at the base of the seal this time. He placed his torch to one side. The light from it falling across him threw weird, wriggling shapes around the chamber as he dug.

Once he was through, a fresh pile of rubble had been scattered across the floor. For a moment there was silence. The carved faces of animals watched from the darkness. The three explorers stood in pools of torchlight, hardly daring to make a sound.

"Well," said Carter at last. "Let's see what's inside, shall we?"

The hole was small. Carter shone his flashlight through to the other side. Reflected back were ancient Egyptian designs, shaped in gold against a vibrant blue.

"Is it made of gold?" said Carnarvon, crouching down as far as his old bones would allow. "What is it? Another wall?"

"No, wood I think," said Carter. "With gold laid over the top. It might be a box, or the side of a large ornament."

"Perhaps we should make a second hole to one side?" said Lady Evelyn. "To get around it?"

Carter lay on his back and pulled himself through the hole up to his shoulders. He coughed as stirred-up dust clung around his face. "I don't think we'll need to," he said. "There's just enough space to crawl through and stand up in." He struggled to twist himself around. "Whatever this is here, it's quite big. I can't feel a corner yet."

"You two go through," said Carnarvon. "I'm feeling as ancient as these **artefacts** meself! Don't think I'd quite make the squeeze."

Carter was already hauling himself through into the blackness beyond. He'd left his torch in the outer chamber.

The gap between the wall-seal and the whatever-it-was was barely half a metre. He groped cautiously to the left. In the pitch black, the tips of his fingers

Head (called a "Bust") of Tutankhamun

felt the wall to one side, the intricate carved surface to the other. Then he felt something on the floor... Loose, round... A jar, perhaps.

He looked over his shoulder. The glow of the torches from the outer chamber flickered and shifted as Lady Evelyn crawled through after him.

"Careful, girl," called Carnarvon. "Priceless relics in there, don't forget!"

"Still treats me like a baby," mumbled Lady Evelyn to herself. After a little struggling, she managed to pull her feet through and stand, next to Carter. She stretched out her arms.

"I can't feel a corner to this object even now," she whispered.

"Neither can I," whispered Carter. "It must be a good five metres wide."

From the outer chamber, Carnarvon pushed two torches through the hole. Carter and Lady Evelyn's faces suddenly flashed in the beams as they were picked up.

On the other side of the wall, Carnarvon sat next to the hole, trying to catch his breath.

"What is it?" he called. He saw the yellowy, glowing torchlight through the hole grow dim as Carter swung his torch up to take a first look.

"Carter? Evelyn?" he called. "What can you see?"

"Eyes!" called Carter. "A pair of eyes!"

Eyes painted on a wooden sarcophagus

Carter's torch shone on the side of the huge object. Large Egyptian eye-designs, placed there to guard against evil, stared back at him, centimetres from his nose.

Lady Evelyn had never felt so frightened in her life. She pressed her back to the wall, and held up her torch. It lit up the whole room.

The Final Room

The burial chamber they were standing in was a similar size to the first room. Where the first room's walls had been bare, the walls in here were decorated with paintings and hieroglyphs. Their colours were bright and fresh, as if the paint had only just dried.

Ancient life and ancient times loomed over them from the walls. To the right, paintings of twelve monkey-gods, representing the twelve hours of the night through which, it was said, the sun had to travel in order to shine again the next day.

Above and ahead of them, pictures of the boy king, Tutankhamun, and the pharaoh who followed him, Ay. In one picture, Tutankhamun was greeted by the goddess Isis and welcomed into the Afterlife. In another, he met Osiris, god of the dead. In another, the dog-headed Anubis, the **embalmer**.

To the left, a scene of the fully mummified king, encased in a wooden shrine. The shrine was on a barge, being pulled by twelve men wearing white, the colour of mourning.

*The ancient Egyptian depiction of
Tutankhamun's funeral ceremony*

The huge object in front of them was that same wooden shrine. It took up almost the entire chamber.

Carter shone his torch along the strip of floor on which the two of them stood. Objects of various kinds had been placed there, as the ancient Egyptians had left the room for the last time, ready to seal it up. There was a wine jar, as Carter had already found, along with boxes made of reed and papyrus, small **figurines** of Osiris, shrivelled-up offerings of food and more.

Osiris shown in an ancient Egptian painting

But it was the shrine that commanded their attention. Carter, his eyes wide, crept his way around the edge of the chamber. Every part of the shrine was decorated in carvings and hieroglyphs, and at one end, near where Lady Evelyn stood, was a pair of low doors.

"Lady Evelyn! Bring your torch!" called Carter. "I need more light!"

Lady Evelyn squeezed around the corner of the shrine and crouched down beside Carter. As the beam of her torch swung around and lit up the space behind him, she let out a terrified gasp.

Carter turned. A dark, long-eared face glared out at them from another doorway, this one unsealed. The statue of a jackal was covered in cloth, and sat on a raised sled.

"The final room," breathed Carter. "The treasury. That's the god Anubis, watching over the dead king."

Anubis, who takes the form of a jackal. He guides the dead into the next world, and was considered to be the inventor of mummification

He turned back to the small doors in the shrine. In front of the doors, on the floor, had been placed a little perfume vessel on a stand, an offering to Tutankhamun. The doors were bolted shut, and marked with the same cartouche of the jackal and nine slaves that they'd seen on the first seal-wall, at the foot of the stone steps.

"Is there anything there?" called Carnarvon.

"The shrine is unbroken," said Carter. "It's complete. It hasn't been opened for over three thousand years."

"So... what's inside this shrine?" said Lady Evelyn.

"Tutankhamun himself," whispered Carter. "Within this shrine there'll be a second shrine, perhaps a third, and inside that, a sarcophagus. And inside that... the mummy of the king. Undisturbed for thousands of years. Lying here, in the silence, in the darkness."

With trembling hands, he pulled back the bolt that held the doors shut.

Story Background

Howard Carter's discovery was one of the greatest finds in history. Once the tomb itself was discovered, every one of the thousands of objects that it contained was recorded and preserved. New information was uncovered about how the ancient Egyptians lived and died.

   This work of sorting and cataloguing was long and painstaking. It was ten years before it was finished! The most amazing treasures were found inside the sarcophagus: the mummy was dressed in intricate jewels and topped with a golden mask. It, like many of Carter's finds, is now in the Museum of Antiquities in Cairo.

The king wasn't very tall, and was only around nineteen years old when he died. It's thought that he may have been murdered, although why isn't known. Perhaps his successor, Ay wanted the throne? In the history of Egypt, Tutankhamun was a relatively minor figure, but with the help of Howard Carter, his name will live forever.

Howard Carter and assistant examining the inner coffin

Index

Glossary

afterlife life after death

annexe an extra building

artefacts man-made objects

cartouche an oval enclosing the name of an ancient Egyptian king

casket a small box for holding valuables

dynasty line of hereditary rulers

electric torches special torches powered by electricity

embalmer one who preserves dead bodies with spices

figurine a small statue

hieroglyphics pictures or symbols representing words or syllables, especially in ancient Egyptian writing

mummified bodies covered in preserving oils and wrapped in cloth

sarcophagus stone coffin